D1519069

CARS

GTO

Michael Bradley

mc Marshall Cavendish
Benchmark
New York

Marshall Cavendish Benchmark
99 White Plains Road
Tarrytown, NY 10591
www.marshallcavendish.us

Library of Congress Cataloging-in-Publication Data

Bradley, Michael, 1962—
  GTO / by Michael Bradley.
      p. cm. — (Cars)
  Includes bibliographical references and index.
  ISBN 978-0-7614-4112-0
  1. GTO automobile—History—Juvenile literature. I. Title.
    TL215.G79B73 2010
    629.222'2—dc22
    2008035966

Editor: Megan Comerford
Publisher: Michelle Bisson
Art Director: Anahid Hamparian
Series Designer: Daniel Roode

Photo research by Connie Gardner

Cover photo by Ron Kimball/www.kimballstock.com

The photographs in this book are used by permission and through the courtesy of:
CORBIS: Transtock, 1; Neil Rabonowitz, 7; Car Culture, 18, Katy Winn, 20; *Alamy*: Paul Collis, 6;
GM Media Archive: 10, 12, 13, 14, 17, 24, 26, 27; *RonKimball/www.kimballstock.com*: Back Cover, 4, 8, 16, 19,
21, 23, 25, 28, 29.

Printed in Malaysia
1 3 5 6 4 2

CONTENTS

The 1964 Pontiac GTO started the muscle car craze in the United States. The cars came in colors like bright red, which made them even more noticeable on the road.

It lasted only ten years, and its final days were sad, thanks to lack of interest and angry **competition**. But for five years, nothing could touch the GTO, the godfather of all **muscle cars** and the coolest thing around.

There were plenty of cars that tried to imitate the GTO. Some had higher sales totals. But the GTO was the first. Pontiac engineers decided to take a regular, midsized car and jam a power-packed engine into it. They added some hot styling on the outside and painted the car eye-catching colors. The finished product was more than just a car. The GTO became one of the first automobiles to **define** its driver. If you bought a GTO, you were edgy and tough and your car had to have major attitude.

A powerful V-8 engine was at the heart of all the 1964 GTOs and made the car popular among drivers who liked to go fast.

From its **debut** in 1964, the GTO had an attitude that drivers couldn't find in any other car. It wasn't designed for comfort or luxury. The "Goat," as some, in a play on its letters, called it, was supposed to be fast and strong. The GTO was originally intended to be a version of the Tempest, Pontiac's quiet, midsized auto. For an additional cost, buyers could add a V-8 engine, special wheels, and a dual **exhaust** system for the more powerful Tempest GTO. But anybody who bought one knew the car had its own **personality**.

For the next five years, the GTO set America on fire. Each year brought another reason to take a close look at the car, if not buy one. Pontiac was trying to create an image as a performance company by building models that did more than just get drivers from Point A to Point B. There had to be some excitement. And driving a GTO was like riding a thrilling roller coaster.

A wide front grille and two stacked headlights gave the GTO an impressive appearance. Imagine seeing this 1965 model pull up next to you!

After it was introduced, the GTO faced a lot of tough competition. The 1967 Corvette 427, the 1967 Belvedere, and the 1971 Roadster were just some of the muscle cars produced by other companies. A 1965 GTO is parked on the far right.

The nation took plenty of notice. Automotive magazines printed **enthusiastic** articles about the GTO and musicians sang about it. The car even appeared on television shows and in movies. When the GTO made its debut in 1964, Pontiac executives hoped to sell 5,000. Twelve months later, more than 32,000 GTOs had been sold. And that was just the beginning.

Pontiac had a winner on its hands. At a time when its parent company, General Motors, was trying to move away from racing, the GTO **convinced** thousands of drivers to floor the **accelerator** and hold on. It was a short ride, because the GTO was gone by 1974, but it made Americans fall in love with the muscle car.

The GTO was so popular that automakers hurried to make a "Goat" of their own. The number of competitors eventually became too much for the GTO. It's a tribute to the GTO that by the 1970s, Ford, Chrysler, Chevy, Plymouth, and just about every other American automaker had its own version on the road. They may have driven the GTO out of production, but they couldn't take its title as the first-ever muscle car.

And they couldn't stop it from being a legend today.

START

John DeLorean stands next to a 1968 Tempest GTO coupe at the starting line of an auto race. DeLorean was a risk-taker, but his gamble on the powerful GTO paid off!

CHAPTER TWO
BIRTH OF A LEGEND

John DeLorean, Pontiac's chief engineer, held meetings called "What If" sessions at the company's test track on Saturdays. DeLorean gathered together sharp minds and asked them to think beyond the usual. He wanted new ideas. He wanted to know not what *had* been done, but what *could* be done.

One day, he was asked what would happen if Pontiac put a growling 396-cubic inch (6.5-liter) engine in the midsized Tempest. Introduced in 1961, the Tempest had excellent handling, but it wasn't a big seller. The idea of cramming a power plant that big into something that normally had a 326-cubic inch (5.3-liter) engine was unheard of. And exactly what DeLorean was looking for. By the next "What If" meeting, just one week later, a pumped-up Tempest was on the track and ready to roll. Little did everybody know that the GTO had been born.

Pontiac engineers sidestepped the rules by first offering the GTO as a special package on Pontiac's Tempest and LeMans. Buyers could upgrade to a more powerful engine to make their Pontiacs GTO models.

At the time, Pontiac was moving away from the professional racing world: It was shifting from the track to the street. The General Motors board had put limits on the amount of power a car could have. But DeLorean and his engineers found a way around that. Their creation wouldn't be a new model. It would be an **options** package on the existing Tempest. Pontiac general manager Pete Estes didn't even tell the GM board about it because he was afraid they wouldn't approve.

The folks at Ferrari weren't too happy with it, either. Pontiac stole the name *GTO* from the Italian carmaker. It stood for "Gran Turismo Omologato," and it meant the car was approved for racing. The Ferrari GTO was. The Pontiac GTO was not. When the Pontiac GTO debuted in 1964, automotive **purists** complained. Those who bought the car didn't care. They loved its power and the cool image it gave them. Young adults not ready to buy "family" cars or boring sedans loved the GTO's edgy look and ability to rock the road.

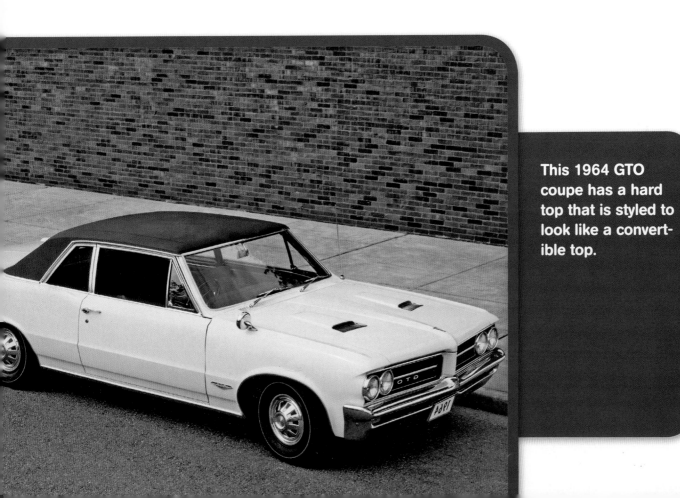

This 1964 GTO coupe has a hard top that is styled to look like a convertible top.

In 1965 GTOs started sporting "Tiger Paw" tires. People decorated their GTOs with tiger-print seatbelts, door panels, and even paint jobs!

Pontiac was careful to introduce the GTO slowly. It began by putting the new car into the hands of drivers who would recognize the power and style of the GTO. That way, a feeling of excitement would build, and people would want in on the new **sensation**. The strategy worked. *Car and Driver* magazine, one of the nation's authorities on the auto world, said the GTO could do anything Ferrari could—for less money. Pontiac had created a car that offered affordable performance to young adults. The GM executives were upset that the GTO took sales from the Chevrolet Corvette, another car in the company's garage, but Pontiac didn't care. It was making history.

It was also making money. GM predicted it would sell 5,000 GTOs, but a whopping 32,450 moved out of showrooms. The word was out. By asking "what if" and then following up on a good idea, Pontiac had made a name for itself in the automotive world. No longer was it a quiet part of GM. It was a performance leader.

The muscle car was born, and the GTO was ready to rumble.

This 1966 GTO is a tiger-inspired orange with black racing stripes and a special license plate that reads "GR-RRR!"

CHAPTER THREE
THE TIGER GROWLS

How cool was the new GTO? Well, in late 1964, surf-rock band Ronny and the Daytonas hit number four on the pop charts with their song, "Little GTO," which praised the new car.

Pontiac latched on to the tiger theme and used it in their advertisements. General Motors wanted to show that the GTO was both beautiful and strong—like a tiger!

The Monkeemobile, featured on the popular TV show *The Monkees*, was a customized 1967 GTO. Pontiac lengthened the body, redesigned the car's nose, and added a GMC 671 blower, which was usually only for race cars. The singing group toured the country in the Monkeemobile.

The country was crazy for the GTO, and the excitement was building. Pontiac didn't want to let the **momentum** die. The 1965 model was lighter, faster, and more powerful. The engine delivered more **horsepower** and was fast enough to race. There were new gauges inside and a sharp interior. But the most important part of the equation was the new tires. The GTO was outfitted with Uniroyal "Tiger Paw" tires. They were thicker, bolder, and added to the car's tough personality.

Now president of Pontiac, John DeLorean understood American youth. He knew image and style were as important as a car's quality. A car expressed the driver's personality. So, GTO's advertising agency grabbed onto the Tiger theme and ran with it. GTO drivers could purchase front license plates that said, "GR-RRR!" Fuzzy tiger tails were tied to radio antennas on GTOs. Sales more than doubled in 1965 to 75,352. It was official: If you were young and cool, you had to have a GTO.

These 1964, 1966, and 1974 GTOs show how Pontiac restyled the car. In 1966 Pontiac introduced a new front grille and a restyled rear window. By 1974, the GTO was smaller, lower to the ground, and had a more streamlined body.

Plenty of automakers felt the pressure to compete with the GTO and, in 1966, the copycats appeared. Oldsmobile had the 442. Chevy pumped out the Chevelle. Dodge built the Charger. But there was only one GTO, and it looked better than ever. The power was still the same, but the **exterior** style was different. The GTO had a beefier look, with a new front **grille** and a rear window that looked like a tunnel going into the car. The Tiger was **prowling** American roadways by the thousands. GTO sales topped out at a record 96,946 cars in 1966.

The country loved it, and the GTO became a star. It was featured on TV shows like *My Three Sons*. Captain Tony Nelson, one of the main

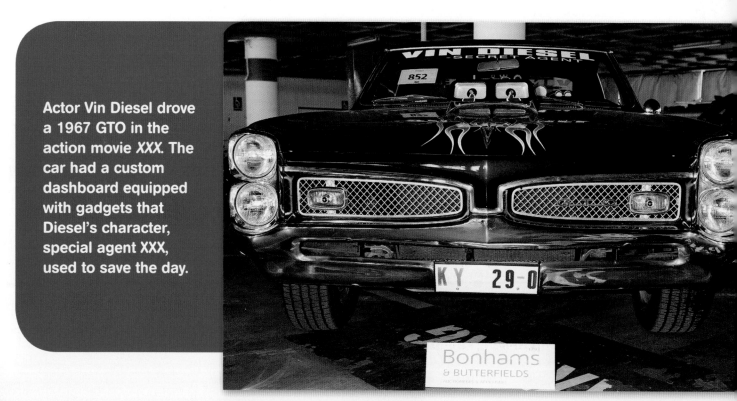

Actor Vin Diesel drove a 1967 GTO in the action movie *XXX*. The car had a custom dashboard equipped with gadgets that Diesel's character, special agent XXX, used to save the day.

Even the engine looks great in a 1967 GTO! Many people who bought GTOs souped up the engines.

characters on *I Dream of Jeannie*, drove a GTO. And Pontiac designed a special 1967 model for The Monkees, a singing group created for what became a popular television show.

Despite growing competition in the late 1960s, the GTO still ruled the muscle car universe. The GTO fan club was growing, and the rest of the automotive world was trying to compete. Though other car companies eventually caught up, spelling trouble for the GTO, the Tiger wasn't done growling just yet.

While Pontiac's rivals were busy designing and perfecting their own muscle cars, the GTO **revamped** its image in 1968. Though some were surprised at Pontiac's decision to redesign the car's exterior, it was a successful move.

The 1968 GTO sported a new, rounder body, but there was no mistaking the GTO's power source, which remained the same—for a few months. In March, Pontiac pumped things up and gave the car even more horsepower. It was the perfect way to keep the car rolling ahead. In fact, 87,684 GTOs were sold, making 1968 the car's second-best sales year.

The country had come to view the top muscle car as a symbol of all things modern and fresh. Max Factor had

"The Humbler" debuted in 1970. Pontiac aired a popular commercial during Superbowl IV to promote the special-edition GTO.

created a GTO cologne and shaving cream for the fashionable, car-loving man. That was still the goal: to make drivers feel that they were cool, exciting, and on the cutting edge.

To drive that theme home, the 1969 GTO introduced another new version: "The Judge." The model was named for a skit on the popular comedy show, *Laugh-In*, in which Sammy Davis Jr. entered the courtroom to the chant, "Here comes the judge!" "The Judge" had stripes, a spoiler, a blacked-out grille, and even "The Judge" stickers on the fenders. The first Judge came in one color, an orangey hue called Carousel Red. But by the end of the year, it was available in all the GTO colors.

In 1969 Pontiac debuted "The Judge" GTO, which was built to be the ultimate street-performance car. For the first several months it was only available in an eye-catching orange color.

Even though it was more expensive than the standard GTO, car enthusiasts loved the special engine, rear spoiler, and stylized wheels on the 1970 "The Judge" model.

"The Judge" helped Pontiac stay strong in the face of fierce competition. Although sales dropped, a respectable 72,287 GTOs were sold. But that was the last time the GTO would be riding high. At the end of 1969, John DeLorean, who had made the creation of the GTO possible, moved on to take over GM's Chevrolet division. His decision to leave was a big blow to Pontiac and left the GTO without a cheerleader in the **boardroom**.

The 1970 version offered a 455-cubic inch (7.5L) V-8 engine option and was nicknamed "The Humbler" because it made other cars seem **inadequate**. Many who bought it liked to make it even more powerful by adding to the engine. The next three years, however, were hard for the GTO as rising insurance costs, tougher U.S. laws on the smoky emissions from muscle cars, and increasing competition hurt sales. In 1973 there were just 4,806 new GTOs on the road. It was no longer cool to be big and loud. Cars from Japan were smaller and more **fuel efficient**. GM executives, who never really liked the car, had an excuse to end its run. In the summer of 1974 the announcement came: The GTO was discontinued.

This 1974 GTO marked the end of an era for Pontiac. The company stopped producing the car in the United States after the 1974 models were released.

GTO

The GTO was brought back in 2004 but looked more like a modern sports car than like the muscle cars of the 1960s. It only lasted two years and very few were sold in the United States.

It made a brief comeback from 2004 to 2006, when it was built by an Australian division of GM, but the cars did not sell well in the United States. The GTO is remembered for its first six years. That's when it set the tone for the muscle car **revolution**. That's when it made a generation of drivers feel cool. The GTO was a trendsetter, and it will always be remembered for its power and imagination.

The Tiger had growled, all right, and America heard it.

Vital Statistics

1964 Pontiac GTO

Power: 325 hp
Engine Size: 389 ci/6.5L
Engine Type: Pontiac V-8
Weight: 3,423 lbs (1,553 kg)
Top Speed: 93 mph (150 km/h)
0–60 mph (0–96.5 km/h): 7.4 sec

1974 Pontiac GTO

Power: 200 hp
Engine Size: 350 ci/5.7L
Engine Type: Pontiac V-8
Weight: 3,376 lbs (1,531 kg)
Top Speed: 88 mph (142 km/h)
0–60 mph (0–96.5 km/h): 7.7 sec

GLOSSARY

accelerator   The pedal beneath the steering wheel a driver pushes with his or her foot to make a car go faster.

boardroom   The place where the most important people of a large company meet to make big decisions.

competition   A contest between people or companies.

convince   To persuade; to cause a person to do something.

debut   The first time something appears in public.

define   To state the meaning of or to determine the qualities and characteristics of something.

enthusiastic   Having or showing intense interest or desire.

exhaust   The pipe in the back or on the side of a car through which fumes and smoke are released from a working engine.

exterior   The outside; the part of something that is seen.

fuel efficient   Using fuel with minimal waste so that the vehicle goes the farthest possible on one gallon.

grille   The front part of a car, usually made of shiny metal, which protects the engine but also provides a sharp look for the vehicle.

horsepower   The unit used to measure an engine's power. The more horsepower (hp), the stronger the engine and the faster a car can travel.

inadequate   Not meeting the needs of a certain person or situation.

momentum   The force created by the onrush of events.

muscle car   A kind of car popular during the 1960s and early 1970s. Muscle cars were known for their speed and featured a large, powerful engine and a bulky frame.

options	The extras that someone can add to a product, such as a car, to make it more special or successful, usually at an extra cost.
personality	A set of individual traits.
prowling	Moving along in a sneaky manner, as if in search of prey.
purist	Someone who sticks to tradition or the original definition of something.
revamp	To remake and improve.
revolution	A big change in the way things are done.
sensation	A cause of excitement.
symbol	A sign of an idea.

FURTHER INFORMATION

BOOKS

DeMauro, Thomas. *Collector's Originality Guide: Pontiac GTO 1964–1974.* St. Paul, MN: Motorbooks, 2008

Statham, Steve. *Pontiac GTO: Four Decades of Muscle.* St. Paul, MN: Motorbooks, 2003.

Zuehlke, Jeffrey. *Muscle Cars* (Motor Mania). Minneapolis, MN: Lerner, 2007.

WEBSITES

www.ultimategto.com
www.gtoaa.org
www.cruisintigersgto.com

Page numbers in **boldface** are photographs.

About the Author

MICHAEL BRADLEY is a writer and broadcaster who lives near Philadelphia. He has written for *Sports Illustrated for Kids*, *Hoop*, *Inside Stuff*, and *Slam* magazines and is a regular contributor to Comcast SportsNet in Philadelphia.